UPON THE JET STREAM

Upon The Jet Stream

Copyright © 2025 by Tethered Wrds.

All rights reserved. No part of this book may be reproduced, stored in a retrieval system, or transmitted in any form or by any means—electronic, mechanical, photocopying, recording, or otherwise—without the prior written permission of the publisher, except for brief quotations in critical reviews or articles.

This work contains an excerpt from *The Wood Between the Worlds: A Poetic Theology of the Cross* by Brian Zahnd, republished with permission from InterVarsity Press through a license agreement with Copyright Clearance Center, Inc. ("CCC"). The license consists of Order License ID 1585052-1, issued on March 5, 2025, for the excerpt from Chapter 8, "What is Truth" (pp. 81-82). All rights remain with InterVarsity Press.

Book design by Elizabeth Bell

ISBN: 979-8-9892453-1-4
Library of Congress Control Number: 2025910595

Learn more at *tetheredwrds.com*.
For inquiries, please contact Tethered Wrds at *connect@tetheredwrds.com*.

This project is funded in part by the South Carolina Arts Commission which receives support from the National Endowment for the Arts.

This project is also funded in part by a generous award from the Expansion Arts Fund of The Coastal Community Foundation of South Carolina.

*To my parents, N.D. and R.D. —
I get my spirit of grit and resilience from you, Mom,
and I understand that words have meaning
from you, Dad. Thank you.*

PROSE & POETRY *by* TETHERED WRDS

UPON THE JET STREAM

WAR, *HOPE,* AND HOW *BEAUTY HEALS*

TABLE OF CONTENTS

INTRODUCTION

04	*Take Flight*
09	*Pre-Flight Checklist*
15	*Upon the Jet Stream I*

CHAPTER ONE

18	*From My Journal (Part 1)*
20	*Our Emmaus Road*
22	*Bouquets*
23	*Upon the Jet Stream II*
24	*Anyone Else?*
25	*Weary*
26	*The Lore and Ballad of Tyrant Kings*
27	*Burn*
28	*Questions Through the Tears*
29	*Suspended*
30	*Aaahhh, MONSTER!*
32	*Thrashing Floor*
33	*Glimmers of Hope*
35	*A Prayer*

CHAPTER TWO

38	*Send Me to Hell*
42	*Keeper of the Cloak*

44	*The Keeper*
46	*I Go*
47	*Look Into My Eyes*
50	*Send Me to Hell (To the Gates)*
54	*Entering Darkness*
57	*A Note on Entering Dark and Heavy Spaces*

CHAPTER THREE

| 64 | *Geopolitics & Poetry* |

CHAPTER FOUR

80	*Welcome to Africa*
85	*Exercising an Amen*
87	*Reigning*
88	*Decision Making Principles*
90	*Living as Exiles Yet Forever Present*
92	*Where Have All Our Elders Gone?*
93	*A Heart Song for Africa*
94	*What is This Feeling?*
97	*A Damn Bubble*
98	*The Refuge of God*
101	*Upon the Heavens*
102	*Gentleness Embodied*
105	*A Veil*
106	*I'm Told This is Where the Nile Begins*
107	*Where Elephants Roam*

109	*The Gift of Hospitality*
112	*On a Wednesday*
114	*On Language, Communication, and Honor*
116	*Bismarck's Story*
120	*An Exchange*
125	*A Dash of Doha, Qatar*
126	*Eww!*

CHAPTER FIVE

132	*Cuba Libre*
135	*A Shift*
136	*Landed*
137	*La Habana*
139	*The Struggle*
140	*There She Was...*
144	*Vapor*
146	*Lessons from Cuba*
149	*Finca Vigía (A Lesson from Hemingway's House)*
152	*Finca Vigía*
157	*Haggles & Hubris*
158	*A Bicycle Seat*
161	*Lessons From a Cuban*

CHAPTER SIX

166	*Ukraine*
170	*Staging Area*

172	*Long Flight*
175	*Flow*
176	*Arrival*
179	*Silence*
181	*Sounds of Somber*
183	*Stories from the Field*
190	*For Roman*
192	*Advice from the Field*
197	*Have You Ever Seen a Tiger Cry?*
204	*The Mercenary with Amber Honey Eyes*
209	*Powerless*
210	*Thinking Out Loud I*
211	*Thinking Out Loud II*
213	*Hey God I*
214	*Hey God II*
217	*Would You Unlearn and Listen?*

CHAPTER SEVEN

222	*From My Journal (Part 2)*
223	*The Language of Eternity*
224	*How Do We Find Peace in the Pieces?*
226	*The Years Have Been Long*
230	*I Beat My Chest!*
232	*In Light of Everything Heavy...*
235	*& Again*
236	*Is it a Win?*

238	*Excerpt from The Wood Between the Worlds*
242	*What's in a Name?*
245	*I Have No Earthly King!*
246	*Fleeting*
248	*Splitting Lightning*
249	*What is Life?*
251	*Would We Dare to Dream Again?*
252	*Fallout*
253	*Mercy*
254	*I Have No Enemies*
256	*Stolen*
258	*Tired*
259	*Overlooked*
260	*Between Spaces*
262	*Memento Mori*
265	*Expiration Dates*
266	*To the Givers of Self*

CHAPTER EIGHT

| 272 | *Beauty Heals* |
| 281 | *Magnificence* |

| 283 | *Thank You* |
| 287 | *Notes* |

THE IBIS — *Wisdom, knowledge and divine communication*

INTRO
TAKE

FLIGHT

INTRO

TAKE FLIGHT

Taking flight grants one a new perspective not available to those who remain grounded—and yet, even birds must land. I've often fantasized about having the power of flight—for the escape, the adventure, the calculated risk, and, of course—the new perspective. Writing this book and piecing together its pages revealed to me that I have been gifted the power of flight in a different form.

Because of this gift, I have traveled and embarked on journeys that few can or are willing to take. The past two years were hard. My transition through ministry, work, the release of relationships, new beginnings, and struggles with faith brought challenges I had never faced before—nor would I ever wish to erase from my history. Through the brokenness and stress, I published my first book, *Threads of Resilience*, and after traveling across seven countries, I find myself writing a second. There is always beauty in brokenness, and I have found that faith is fortified in trying times. The flights I've taken to meet people in distant lands helped to heal many of those wounds. There were times I was the one on the outside looking in—feeling and listening as an outsider—yet was taken in and loved as one of their own.

Within these pages, you'll find the journeys I've taken, but not everything is written. First, I believe some stories are meant only for the one who experienced them—not everything needs to be shared. It's okay to hold treasured things close.

Second, not everything can be conveyed through writing. I don't yet know how to help you connect, but maybe, if we meet, something will spill over in conversation.

Lastly, while these may seem like adventures, they are not meant to be shared as mere adventures. The poems and reflections in this book are tethered to real and difficult situations—to extraordinary lives, breathtaking places, and remarkable people—more than a mere steward of stories can ever do justice. I never want my sense of adventure or risk-taking to come at the expense of someone else's reality. The stories, poems, and images I share are intentional. I hope they inspire you on your own journey and honor those whose names will remain only in memory. May the stories shared across these pages instill dignity and hope in these dark and trying times.

I never expected to make it to Africa—and yet, I did. I learned a little more about resilience, hope, and forgiveness from the Africans I met. I also learned how to be okay with not having an answer.

I never expected to witness the wonder of Havana, Cuba. Looking back, I am reminded that I am always learning, growing in humility, and unlearning much. Proximity builds empathy, and perspectives must be formed beyond conventional understanding.

I never expected to bear the weight of war in Ukraine—and I put that mildly. To behold both beauty and pain, to be loved by a people, and to be shown hospitality by those who are fighting to receive the same.

I don't know if you hold in your hands something new in the realm of literary compilations, or if I'm at the whim of Apollo (no, I don't believe in Greek mythology), but I've written poetry, prose, and some geopolitical narratives looking to build the undercurrent of this book. It's a book on war, hope, and how beauty heals. It tells stories of the weaving of humanity. *We are not separate people, separate nations, separate worlds*—no matter what politics, borders, or worldviews would have you believe. This isn't globalist talk either, I've just witnessed too much and have crossed thresholds in a way that, from my current perspective, lends to more in life and an interconnectedness that should allow for human flourishing.

I hope to weave a thread of connection across these nations—that through these words, you might take flight upon the jet stream and be carried across borders of lands you may otherwise never step foot upon. May your mind's eye gain a new perspective, may your spirit be stirred to take flights of its own, and may your heart land ever so gently to allow empathy and compassion to take root.

PRE-FLIGHT CHECKLIST

A reflective pause before takeoff

Before you take flight, *breathe.*

As I've stated, not everything I experienced could be captured with ink and not everything you're about to read will be comfortable. So before you journey through the reflections ahead, take a moment to sit with your own thoughts.

On the next page is a set of questions—a kind of *pre-flight checklist* for the heart and soul. These questions hold space for conversations—a thread to hold as you cross into other lives, other stories.

Take this *Selah* moment to allow your soul to sit in the tension and consider what it's willing to engage... or risk.

PRE-FLIGHT CHECKLIST

- When was the last time I truly listened to a story not my own—without judgment or the urge to fix it?

- Have I confused sympathy with empathy? What would it look like to walk beside, rather than ahead of someone else's pain?

- What are my unspoken assumptions about migration, borders, or who "deserves" to cross? Whose voices shaped those assumptions—and have I ever heard the voices on the other side of the line?

- Who have I labeled as a stranger? What does it mean to offer belonging rather than just welcome?

- When I hear an unfamiliar language or encounter a story that challenges my own—do I lean in with curiosity, or pull back with discomfort? What is it in me that resists what I don't understand? Am I willing to let someone else's truth expand my own?

- How would I change by choosing to see people through the lens of shared humanity rather than difference? What keeps me from seeing the divine—or even the familiar—in them?

- What stories have shaped my sense of right and wrong? Are those stories serving love?

- What does hope look like when everything around it feels heavy?

- What role does faith play in my response to injustice? Is it a comfort, a call to action, or both?

- What am I willing to unlearn in order to truly see another person?

- How does poetry invite me to slow down and feel, rather than just analyze or consume?

UPON THE JET STREAM I
//

You can find me upon the jet stream
fighting dragons.
Upon the seas wrestling krakens.
Gasping, spitting,
reeling, biting;
the tales of Heaven
aren't told by those who take no risk,
who risk the wonder of eternity
for the comfort of today.
I am no hero nor have the hubris
to lord over another, but as a steward of stories
and student of Jonah;[1]
I will no longer allow myself and others
to find themselves in the bellies of Leviathan.

CH. 01

FROM MY

JOURNAL

PART 1

CH. 01

FROM MY JOURNAL

I begin with poetry, as this has become a native tongue—my practice of capturing stories, curating my questions, and forming my awareness of the spiritual.

This chapter is part one of my journal. Though the poems have been written across different flights and locations, I've placed a set of them here in chapter one to lead your mind and heart into my space. Would you hear my heart, feel my hurt and frustration, and understand a little more of my process?

I don't shy away from faith, as I believe faith to be a foundation for life—a bedrock for withstanding the gravity of existence, especially in the realm of the unknown and the darkness that overtakes many. I don't shy away from asking questions. In my personal journals, you'll find prayers and honest moments. But even more intimately, I hope that the poems in my journals help you understand that those who lean into the mystery of life do end up seeing more. And while there may be more questions than answers, there is something wonderful and liberating in allowing yourself to be whisked away by the Spirit of God[1]—carried in moments of despair by His wings, wrapped in protection by His arms.

Poetry and prose are the only ways I can express what I hear and see from God, especially when I bear witness to the lives and narratives of so many beautiful people across the globe. I don't know what your background is, and this journal—these poems—aren't meant to proselytize. But what I can assure you of is that I'll be honest about what I've seen, what I've heard, and where I've been. In my experience, the Spirit of God is always on the move, and within these pages, I'm sure you'll witness these invisible movements as you would a spring breeze.

OUR EMMAUS ROAD
//

I'm not so bold to say I've got the answer
but I've got a multifaceted perspective—
a collection of stories and diverse interactions.
Journey with me, even just briefly,
you never know
it could end up being
our Emmaus Road.[2]

BOUQUETS
//

Life has handed me a bouquet—
stories represented by the flora
in every stem & petal,
thorn & brier,
seemingly dead seed.
Your story is worthy of preservation
and the pressure under the weight of your unfolding
is not your undoing,
it's proof that even dried flowers hold their essence;
beauty, hope & lasting substance.

UPON THE JET STREAM II
//

I'm making moves upon the jet stream
Spirit filled, Spirit led
movements of otherworld fluidity.
I've met with the ravens & ibis
conversations of transcendence.
I've been carried by Pegasus
and humbled by God's presence.

ANYONE ELSE?
//

Anyone else tired of the fight?
Why is it so damn hard to safeguard life?
When did every conversation about human flourishing
become such a struggle?

Why when I ask "why?"
does it end up in a quarrel?

I'm tired not yet worn,
I'm tender not yet torn,
I'm persevering for my soul is preserved
and while my spirit's moving a little slower
I will not succumb to slumber.

Still—

is anyone else tired of the fight
or do I stand alone?

WEARY
//

Weary from the warnings
done with distressing images
traumatized by traumatic content—
anger, fear, death,
the world is gripped in anguish—
how much smaller can our circles get?

THE LORE & BALLAD OF TYRANT KINGS
//

Tired tales of mortals' wars
tyrant kings, ballads and renowned lore.
A cycle of humanity tethered to days of old
tragedies and dramas in perpetuity.
Would the peace of God speak audibly—
stay our hands and steady our hearts,
clear our minds and open our eyes,
wash our souls with divine tears.
When divine tears wash our souls
our eyes are opened and our minds are cleared
our hearts are steadied and our hands unburdened.
When God speaks audibly—
peace reels in the drama and tragedies
perpetuated in humanity's cycle.
The lore and ballad of tyrant kings
and the wars of mortals are laid to rest.

BURN
//

Some men wish to see the world burn,
little do they recognize that fire brings life.
Out of the ashes & renewed soil
seeds of justice & righteousness
will take root—
for the sowers of peace
will continue to walk the earth
tilling hearts, minds & souls.

QUESTIONS THROUGH THE TEARS
//

Are tears not a universal sign?
Are cries not a universal language?
How dare we shut our eyes & ears,
close ourselves off from humanity,
choose sides by creating more borders & walls
for fear of poking the apple of God's eye?
Is the shimmer & twinkle not the Christ?
Did he not cry out for forgiveness?
Did he not shed his own blood
so we would not spill each others'?
Are there no good persons left
willing to lay aside all for the sake of another?

SUSPENDED
//

The world is heavy
suspended between chaos & the insane
Sudan, Afghanistan
Israel, Gaza & Maine.
Protesters being arrested
migrants sitting in cages, detained.
Social media algorithms
will never numb the pain,
nor should it.

We've been dulled by narcissism,
We've been numbed by comfort,
We've been high on toxic positivity
causing others to reel in disgust.

Mental Health continues to
claim many, never realizing
we've become patients.
Idols & false gods are deteriorating
while attempting to drag our souls
to hell.

Aaahhh, Monster!

I'm told the world sits
  at a degree of 23
    meaning we're all set askew.
      looking at each other sideways
        this is our natural view.
         windows over time
           no longer needing reflections
           brokenness was our norm
           and help was the call
         no one ever made.
         pride, fear, narcissism
          kept us in bondage to ourselves
         and we can't muster up the courage
      to fight the monsters within
    so we scream, "Monster!"
at everyone else.

THRASHING FLOOR
//

With billowed breath
I cast curses upon the waters
may they be carried to the depths
known only to leviathan
that he would thrash upon the floor
& crush the burdens
I no longer wish to hold.

GLIMMERS OF HOPE
//

I've released lanterns to the evening sky
holding prayers, thoughts & emotions,
hoping these burning moments
will become stars
against the darkness,
reminding me there's always
glimmers of hope.

This was a conversation
or some would call a prayer—
that I had with Jesus at the
end of 2023 and entering 2024.

Jesus, its been a hard year.

This I know all to well. Would you allow me to carry you, in preparation for what I have in store?

Where else will I go?

The thing is, you always have an answer for everyone else. And truly you believe it well, but would you believe that you are enough and believe me for yourself?

CH. 02
SEND ME

TO HELL

MY MISSION INTO DARK
AND HEAVY PLACES

CH. 02

SEND ME TO HELL

As my calling and mission[1] in life expanded beyond my understanding and borders, I encountered many who were tired of chaos, worn by narratives of death, disenchanted by rhetoric of oppression, and disgusted by systems that perpetuate anything less than dignity.

The road is treacherous, the path has become narrow, but those who lean into the unknown have seen darkness laid bare in shame and life restored through hope.

Upon such roads, I've met a remnant reinstating dignity, embodying compassion, collaborating to transform communities, and showing true courage in a world of falsehood and cowardice.

If you know me, you know I strive in everything to speak life, inspire dignity, and do good. I have found myself bridging worlds by reimagining what could be—thus laying foundations that will build a future of hope, dignity, and life.

As a first responder chaplain,[2] I've been honored to serve alongside EMTs, police, firefighters, and nurses, caring for families in dire and dark circumstances. I've also been called upon to serve those who give of themselves to serve others. These spaces have prepared me to be a covering of protection and renewal. It's a calling I don't take lightly, yet I engage proudly.

Some are drawn to light—to spaces of comfort and certainty. I make this point not to shame or diminish that need, but I have always been drawn to the edges—where pain, conflict, and the weight of the human story press heavy. Not out of recklessness, but out of a deep, calculated understanding that some things must be witnessed, some burdens carried, and some voices amplified by being present.

I was raised to do hard things, to step forward when others step back. My faith is not one of sentimentality but of a raw, unshaken belief in the grit of goodness—the kind that weathers storms, steps into the fire, and still proclaims hope.

Now, I don't walk alone. My foundation and circle of support are small and strong—built by those who believe in this work. I have places of refuge that allow me to rest and recalibrate. I thank Jesus for my chaplaincy training and for building my resilience through experiences over time. I'm grateful for the places of displacement I've stepped into and that my heart hasn't become insensitive to suffering; rather, it has built within me a gut fortitude that keeps me whole and aware of the rawness of life.

So, in full confidence, knowing both who I am and *Whose I am*, I step forward. I step into the darkness, not because I am fearless, but because I have learned that fear bows to purpose—namely, faith. And greater still, it is laid bare before the One who is shrouded in darkness, for He sees and knows all.

I look into the face of Jesus and say, even with a shaky voice—*send me to hell*. For if there is light to be carried, it must go where darkness reigns and where the embrace of comfort is needed on the coldest of nights.

KEEPER OF THE CLOAK

I'm often asked what a chaplain is or does, especially in the last couple of years as I stepped away from being a local church pastor and fully embraced this calling. That question inspired this poem. Within its framework there is some history, and I encourage you to read about *Saint Martin of Tours*.[3]

Compassion & Mercy,
Servanthood & Humility,
Strength & Peace in Crisis.

Wisdom & Discernment,
Intercession & Advocacy,
Hope & Resilience.

**THIS IS WHAT IT MEANS
TO BE A CHAPLAIN.**[4]

THE KEEPER
//

Lord, I have no desire
to be a "keeper of the cloak"
but to give mine away.
Sew within my sinewed heart and mind
a spiritual garment that allows me to be present
thus becoming a living cloak
in life's obscure moments.

Let me pull Heaven to Earth,
and become a covering of embrace and
protection whispering peace upon a person:
"I am here, the good King sent me."

I GO
//

I go to hell so you don't have to.
Jesus went to Hades
so we don't have to.
We take on the ills so you don't have to
bear it alone & feel the full weight of disaster
and since I follow my Father's voice
walk along the road of Brother's choice,
victorious I rise.
Hand in hand
arms over shoulders
smoke filled lungs
smirks with smolders
cuz I don't fear death—
for me, this side of life is already eternal
Jesus paid it all
so I swipe his black card.

LOOK INTO MY EYES
//

I've got stories of storming the gates.

I've got mason jars preserving the weight

Of tears & laughter.

I am but a steward of stories

Presenting you with life's precious moments.

I am a bearer of good news:

Hold my hand,

Grab my shirt,

Add another rip in my jean jacket.

"Look into my eyes—

I'm here for you."

I wrote this poem in a Shakespearean style rather than my typical free verse. It's a six-part piece with a play on heroic rhyme scheme in ABABCC.

Send Me to Hell

SEND ME TO HELL
(TO THE GATES)
//

I. THE CALL
Send me to the depths where shadows crawl,
For light will pierce what darkness hides.
I fear no demon's name, no ancient thrall,
Their fury falters; their rage subsides.
The gates may quake, the chains may groan,
But Heaven whispers, "You are not alone."

II. THE DESCENT
Through ashen winds and fires that singe,
I march where hope is seldom found.
Each step, a spark, a holy hinge,
That swings on faith's unyielding sound.
Let demons shriek, let curses fly—
Their reign is fleeting; so too, they'll die.

III. THE BATTLE

They rise like storms, their claws like knives,
But truth unmasks their hollow core.
For death itself no longer thrives,
Its sting is broken forevermore.
Though fear may bloom, it cannot stay,
For I am forged of dawn's first ray.

IV. THE PURPOSE

Not for my glory, Lord, nor for my gain,
Upon this journey with steady tread.
For every heart that beats in pain,
For souls the world has left for dead.
Though scars may carve my body deep,
The love I bear will never sleep.

V. THE TRIUMPH

And when the gates are shattered wide,
The trembling earth will cease its groan.
The fallen angels, forced to abide,
Will bow before He who is known.
Let Heaven come, let justice swell—
For The Son's true love shall not be quelled.

VI. THE ASCENSION

Send me to Hell,
For at my back is Heaven's strength,
And hope within billows forth as sails.
I am but mortal, with grit of faith—
Rising on eagles' wings,
Battle-torn, body worn, my soul sings.

ENTERING DARKNESS
//

When have you allowed yourself
To be shrouded in darkness?
To hide in mystery,
To watch over the chaos and void,
Yet remain constant?

When have you stepped into the abyss,
Allowing yourself
To be enveloped in the obscure?
To feel the weight of death upon your shoulders,
And begin to buckle under its pressure?

When have you seen the unseen?
Heard the unheard?
And the only cleansing outcry
Was that of your lungs ushering forth
A trumpeting voice to scream, "JESUS!?"
To understand in that moment the invitation to
"Be still and know"?

We are called to carry our cross.
We are called to come alongside
And bear burdens,
To be light and salt,
Balms of healing, for in our presence,
We present the God of comfort,
The Prince of Peace, the muzzler of destruction,
And strangler of death.

When was the last time
Your grit of faith was pressed—
Allowing the scent and oil of heaven
To flow through you,
Pouring upon another in need
Of mercy and grace?

We are privileged to introduce the champion,
To watch in childlike wonder the master at hand,
A true companion; it's a fascinating dichotomy
To come alongside him and step aside to behold.

Contra Tenebras — *against the darkness*

A Note On Entering Dark & Heavy Spaces

Borderlands and borders are magnets—places where the kingdom of darkness lingers. Many demonic beings have made these spaces their home. Drawn to desperation and brokenness, they feed on suffering—amplifying despair and manifesting spiritual afflictions as physical symptoms in those seeking Hope and Light.

The spirit world's influence is evident—not just in our interactions, but in the very policies that shape the physical realm. The words we speak can be echoes from the shadows, binding human beings, image-bearers of God, to suffering and torment at the hands of evil.

Some knowingly give in to these insidious forces, but many do so unknowingly by failing to stand as protectors or by remaining silent when others need a voice.

For those who would relinquish all to grab hold of the Kingdom of Light to which Jesus extends, know this: the kingdom of darkness salivates at the chance to devour souls and continue the chaos between all.

Yet, Hope is never lost!

PASTOR DAVID KITE
GRACE CITY CHURCH
CHARLESTON, SC[5]

"Chaos is often—*if not always*—the prelude to God's movement."

CH. 03

GEO-
POLITICS

& POETRY

THREADS ACROSS CONTINENTS

CH. 03

GEOPOLITICS & POETRY

As I stated in the introduction, this book is not about borders—at least, not in the way we are taught to see them. I'm reiterating that point here because, as this chapter unfolds, you will see how universal themes play out across seemingly individual nations and the confinement within man-made lines.

These pages hold an undeniable truth: *we are not separate people, separate lands, or separate worlds*, no matter what politics or self-serving history would have us believe. And yet, we are distinct—unique people on unique lands, shaped by unique contexts of life.

At the risk of sounding naïve or repetitive, this isn't globalist rhetoric, nor am I seeking to teach history or take political sides. I have simply seen too much and stepped between too many worlds. My poetry captures weighty subjects, but in this narrative, I seek to unfold a rich history without requiring you to sift through symbolism and layered meanings.

My hope in writing this chapter is twofold. First, that you come to understand more clearly how connections stretch across landscapes—beyond mainstream ideologies, beyond the imposed separations of maps and history. Through a blend of poetry and my iteration of geopolitical narratives, I seek to build the following undercurrent—to show that while *war divides, hope persists,* perhaps in ways you haven't heard before.

Secondly, I hope you recognize that the weaving of humanity is not an abstract concept; it is tangible, lived, and undeniable. It is different from how we view it from afar or read about it in books, yet deeply relatable. I won't deny that you may find yourself provoked to rethink what you thought you knew—or better yet, inspired to learn more.

I begin with a historical moment when Cuba rose as an unexpected ally on the African continent, offering a narrative far removed from the fear-mongering, enemy-of-the-state propaganda we Americans are so often fed.

I first heard of Cuba's involvement in Africa from Cubans themselves. Then, I stumbled upon a historical paper on this overlooked piece of world history in a small, forgotten nook of Spanish stone—a bookstore off the beaten path. Had I not been in Africa only a few months earlier, I would have never been able to relay my journey, my stories, and the lessons I learned. Now, here in the Pearl of the Antilles, I am discovering a connection between these two distant worlds.

From there, I lead you to South Sudan, where the thread of war and the struggle for independence further interlace this tapestry.

Finally, we enter into the ongoing war in Ukraine, a conflict that echoes the struggles of the past while shaping an uncertain future.

Structurally, I transition through these historical narratives with poetry to offer an added layer for internalizing the themes of connection and solidarity. We must move beyond analysis and into something felt and lived.

* * *

It's 1975 and in the heart of war-torn Angola, where oppression casts a long shadow, Cuba extended its hand.

Operation Carlota[1] wasn't just a military intervention: it was a declaration of solidarity. Thousands of Cuban soldiers crossed the ocean, not as conquerors, but as comrades—lifting up a people who had long been crushed under the weight of colonialism and imperialism.

In that distant land where the cries of the oppressed echoed through the mountains and plains, Cuba's soldiers found strangers turned brothers in the fight for liberation. Together, they energized a shift in history, not with force alone, but with the power of shared purpose. Only a decade earlier, Che Guevara disappeared into the Congo in support of the rebels—another example of that sentiment.

Though small, Cuba stood tall
From the Caribbean to open sea
Closing the gap and lifting those on their knees.

These historical moments and interwoven narratives were born from a collective struggle of oppressed people. This intervention by Cuba was a reminder of what solidarity can achieve. Their involvement wasn't just strategic; it was a deep, human commitment to the ideals of freedom and justice, some would call it internationalism.

For Cuba, it was never about planting a flag or their own political victory—it was about lifting others to victory. Russia wasn't even notified of Cuba's involvement. Cuba had a defiance against The Powers and The Goliaths of the world that said, "We will not back down and we will not forsake others."

Operation Carlota—
Not just a name but a movement.
Not just a name but a promise of defiance.
Not just a name but a reminder of unity.

In the shadows of global power struggles, Cuba's intervention illuminated the path toward collective liberation. It was a testament to what happens when people come together across borders, when they see each other not as distant "others" but as part of the same struggle.

Across the oceans and through the battlegrounds, the message was clear: oppression is not an isolated wound. It is a collective scar, and the fight to heal belongs to us all. Cuba's soldiers in Angola became more than defenders of a nation—they became symbols of a revolution that does not know boundaries, a revolution that understands only one truth: that lifting another is the truest form of freedom.

Now we enter our modern day— the World received its newest country in 2011.

In *First Raise a Flag: How South Sudan Won the Longest War but Lost Peace*,[2] the author chronicles the remarkable and painful journey of South Sudan from its roots to the harsh reality of post-independence conflict. The book delves into the struggles of one of the longest civil wars and, in my opinion, proves how imperialism and colonialism undergirds a spirit of angst and strife. I understood the history related in that book by listening to the stories of refugees and sitting with these beautiful people. Again, textual knowledge with testimonies allowed me to understand the struggles and joys of South Sudan's history.

While eventually South Sudan would form, the people of South Sudan would find themselves trapped in a cycle of internal violence, political corruption, and ethnic divisions that undermined the promises of peace that independence symbolizes.

For decades they fought for this very moment,
A flag to raise, a nation to be birthed.
But victory is not peace
And freedom is not the end of war.

Victory and tragedy are woven throughout this book, and in my limited understanding, form a consistent thread in many of the stories across the African Continent. Refugees in Northern Uganda and people I met in South Sudan relayed stories of their fight for freedom and liberation from oppressors. They spoke of their inner wrestling to breathe anew and become more than what another says you are or expects you to be. They shared the raw struggles of bringing lasting peace and an inclusive government. A strife which led to a devastating civil war and reminded the world that while freedom may be attained, it is only but a first step.

Building a nation capable of sustaining freedom requires more than the absence of violence—it requires unity, trust, and an unwavering commitment to peace.

A flag raised in joy
Yet from behind it, shadows stir—
For peace is not born from the silence of weapons,
But from the strength of shared souls.

Traveling from South Sudan to Uganda and Cuba allowed honest moments of clarity. The inability to heal can lead to divisions, complex emotions, and deep wounds.

These countries are not alone.

I bore witness to diminishing hope and frustration across the landscape of Eastern Ukraine.

How much more can we ask for?
How much louder can we shout?
How big of a sacrifice must be made
To the god of war so that life is no longer snuffed out?

In the context of the ongoing conflict in Ukraine (as of the writing of this book), we can read and witness South Sudan's experience and apply some of the same themes and sentiments: national sovereignty, the cost of war, fragile humanity, waning spirits, and the fight for peace.

Just as South Sudan fought for independence only to face a devastating internal war soon after; just as outside pressure and governments affect alliances and networks in Cuba; just as the testing of resilience and support plays out in neighboring countries like Uganda, so too, Ukraine is experiencing these realities.

The invasion has pressed into every aspect of life, stretching the capacity of every individual. Ukraine will have to breathe deep and reinvigorate a country worn from isolation—nation from nations, and men from families.

A nation born from struggle,
Yet still fights for freedom, yes—
But greater still for the right to stand,
The right to belong and have their own motherland.

The price of peace for any nation is the labor of rebuilding not just the country, but the hearts and minds of its people. There's no need to find ourselves alone; the people of Earth should find kin and friendship in their neighbors, for we all struggle against oppressors and those looking to bind any and all human beings.

Peace is not won on battlefields
It is birthed from unity,
It is forged in the willingness and fire
That says, we and future generations deserve more.

History has been ugly, but my hope in connecting these themes of resilience and honesty is that we find ourselves on the side of history that stands with another, particularly the most vulnerable of our humanity.

Empathy is built through proximity. The tension of what we experience—what life is versus what it could be—must be changed through courageous vulnerability.

**War divides, hope persists,
and beauty heals, but know this—
there is beauty in the brokenness.**

Across every continent & every country,
The most beautiful of people
Have reshaped the brokenness through tears, smiles,
Laughter and community.

In the darkness there is always a remnant
Holding a resistance and resilience
That relishes a fight against all tyrants.

AFRICAN FISH EAGLE — *Power, strength, freedom and lifelong devotion*

CH. 04
WELCOME

ð
TO AFRICA

SOUTH SUDAN, UGANDA,
A DASH OF DOHA

CH. 04

WELCOME TO AFRICA

When I think of Africa in its current state, when I study its history through books and firsthand accounts, I see a continent that nations and outsiders have continuously taken from. Few truly engage with it, care for it, or see it as an equal partner. So when I examined my own feelings and desires toward Africa, I had to confront an uncomfortable truth: I, too, wanted something from it. The difference was that my desire wasn't for its resources or lands, but for the adventure it promised. I wanted the National Geographic experience—the Big Five of the safari, the thrill of uncharted landscapes, the rush of an adrenaline junkie's dream. Its otherworldliness spoke to my spirit of curiosity.

But as I deepened my understanding of cultural awareness, immigration, and refugee advocacy over the years—as I refined my approach to engagement and grew in empathy—my longing for Africa shifted. No longer was it about adventure and risk. Instead, I found myself asking: *Could*

Africa have something to teach me? I became inspired by the faith of African Christians, the resilience of its people, the richness of its cultures, and beauty. Africa was still a world away, but I had gained a newfound respect for her.

Then the day came. Call it maturity, call it a shift in spirit, but something in me aligned with the path that would finally lead me to Africa. Originally, I planned to make the trip in October 2022, but the night before my departure, an Ebola outbreak shut Uganda off from the world, forcing us to postpone.

I finally traveled here in April 2023. This was a treasure, as I witnessed something extraordinary—the christening of a flagship church that would serve as a hub for education, clean water, vocational training, and medical support. People from various tribes traveled for days to celebrate the completion of this project, a testament to their unity and perseverance.

Our journey to this vast continent took us through Qatar, then down to Uganda, where we boarded a small propeller plane heading north before finally driving into South Sudan. I entered this world as a student, observing how international partnerships[1] function, how communication adapts to the unforgiving African terrain, what civil war truly means for those living through it, what tribal conflict looks like through the eyes of survivors, and how the UN[2] moves and provides support.

Unlike my usual roles—translating, leading teams, managing schedules—this time, I was an outsider. I learned to follow, and to understand only what was translated or shared with me.

The languages, the people, and the breathtaking beauty of Uganda and South Sudan defy description. No photograph could ever do them justice. I was in awe of both the land and its people.

Of course, there were difficult moments, even dangerous ones. At the border town of Nimule, our visas and passports were held for ransom, forcing us to pay extra just to retrieve them. Our real payment, however, was in time—waiting endlessly under the guise of "processing." If not for the powerhouse Sudanese women traveling with us, I can't say how the situation would have ended.

I leave you with reflections, pictures, and poetry from my time in the Motherland.

I was nervous—this was the first time I'd be traveling such a great distance, leaving behind my firstborn and only child for so long. As storms rolled through South Carolina, my thoughts ran wild. Was it just nerves, or was this a sign that I shouldn't go? This piece is both a prayer and a raw expression of emotion.

EXERCISING AN AMEN
//

Storm to my south
that's physical,
storm to my north
that's mental,
I can run from hurricane rains
but the thoughts & anxiety
running 'round my brain
haunt me—
I've gagged the ghouls,
I've silenced the howlers
but things still go bump in the night.
Holy Father awaken your Holy Spirit
and may it be that he is
the only Ghost to roam my house.
Amen.

I ran into passport and visa issues the week before my departure—I couldn't believe I was getting these notifications so close to leaving. After countless calls, I had no choice but to fly to D.C. to sort out my documentation.

REIGNING
//

an interesting thought crossed my mind
as I crossed the reflecting pool—
here I am in my Nation's Capital
getting permission to accomplish the task
given to me by my King;
it seems that Caesar still attempts
to reign supreme,
but Jesus has other dreams!

A Couple Thoughts on My Decision Making Principles

Faithfulness & obedience—
these are the basic principles
of living on mission
with purpose & intention,
sowing into righteousness with good deeds;
safety & security are never determining factors
for Kingdom living,
sacrifice is.

Do all that's within your power to do—
God will handle the rest.

LIVING AS EXILES
YET FOREVER PRESENT
//

Here I lay—
hours before I drive to the nation's capital
reading *Postcards from Babylon*.[3]

Here I stand—
in Washington on the steps of the Lincoln Memorial
overlooking ponds, parks & obelisks.

Here I ponder—
how to live in a modern day Rome
as one of Heaven's own,
a citizen of New Jerusalem,
engaged in proper worship
so that my King Jesus not caesar
is glorified and all creatures great and small
recognize that His banner over us is love
not red, white and blue.

Here I see—
religion has become politics
the constitution has become scripture
ballot boxes are the offering plates.

Here I go—
off to a world where no one has a home
where their reliance is truly on faith and
Christ alone.
While we live as exiles
fighting the war of words and ideologies,
they live as exiles fighting the wars of swords
knowing that they will return
to an awaiting death;
but they live not for kingdoms that come and go,
rise and eventually fall,
but a Kingdom of Heaven that will return on
the train of an Eternal King.

Here I am—
Spirit lead me.

WHERE HAVE ALL OUR ELDERS GONE?
//

Politics aside & over the top honoring
I walked in a procession,
I stood in celebration,
I clapped in jubilation
at the persons in charge
of rebuilding this African nation
pouring the foundation for the next generation
speaking life & encouragement.

Politics aside & over the top honoring
I look at America's history
at this current and future generation
asking myself, "where have all our elders gone?"

A HEART SONG FOR AFRICA
//

Africa, oh Africa
How oft you are thought of as other worldly
broken & beneath "me"—
a land of third world countries
tribal & civil wars,
poverty & atrocities.

Africa, oh Africa
raped of resources
manipulated through many handshakes
seen as exotic yet never loved truly.

Africa, oh Africa
a continent with such vastness of Earthly beauty
I've come to believe
you are the front porch for Heaven's glory.

WHAT IS THIS FEELING?
//

Diaspora—
most don't have this word in their vocabulary.
But here I fly upon westerly winds,
to visit a continent that has shaped the diverse
genetics within me.

My blood ties stem from the bloodshed in Africa,
spilled and carried across the ocean,
to the Caribbean soil of Puerto Rico.

I'm flying back
to what some call the motherland.
No, I'm not staking a claim one way or another,
but I am stating this:
the diaspora of my heritage feels
a little more whole, a little more gathered,
as African soil collects at my feet—
it's grounding.

A DAMN BUBBLE
//

We are so far removed
from
the
reality
of
global
conflict—
we
live
in,
A Damn Bubble.

THE REFUGE OF GOD
//

We read powerful passages,
great truths of God's safety,
His protection,
His mighty arm of salvation—
but do we truly know?
How can we understand?
We are buffered and safeguarded,
self-comforted in every aspect of Western living;
even the blessings and gifts of God
become walls that keep
the very Giver boxed away.
What is the refuge of God?
I listen to the stories of South Sudanese women—
pain real as the earth beneath them, yet joy rises.
The hope of heaven shines in their eyes,
His coming kingdom glistens in their tears.
UN camps and slums, side by side,
await greater glory.

What is the refuge of God?
I wrestle with this question
 as I stand among black-bodied warriors,
 with ivory smiles and gentle voices, they tell me:
"I hope you will only ever wonder,
 for our lives bear the scars of knowing."

UPON THE HEAVENS
//

To mount up and fly upon Pegasus.
To hunt with Orion through the land of the
Great Bear.
To battle against Leo & Draco
courage in my breast as I'm flanked by
Gemini & Sagittarius.
To swim past Pisces
through the waters of Aquarius.
Cygnus & Aquila
Fly over celestial dust.
To tread where few mortals have led
and gaze upon the dwellings of angelic beings—
that is a life worth living.
Stevenson would rise
to read my stories,
Lewis would create trilogies
upon hearing of my journeys.
"To heaven, to heaven"
is my constant plea
As I gaze upon the Southern Cross.

Gentleness Embodied

How could such harsh conditions
create such gentle souls?

The Dinka people are proud
and truly remarkable—
gentleness embodied.

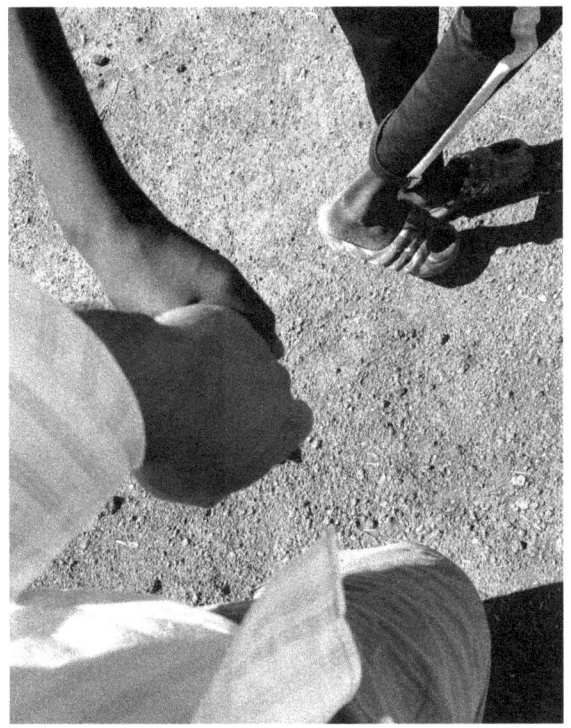

I walked with some of the youth and they showed me their homes and the beauty of the land. I cherished their desire to just share stories, laugh, and play. It didn't matter that we didn't speak each other's language. We held hands and they pointed at their surroundings sharing all they could.

Charcoal making and logging is a huge industry for Uganda. In many areas, and even as we flew over woodlands and forests, you could see the off-white smoke waft about.

A VEIL
//

Red clay soil
Wood smoke & charcoal
A veil of lace dances across a pointillist sky.

I'M TOLD THIS IS WHERE THE NILE BEGINS
//

Murchison Falls
The roar of the Nile
Your voice is powerful
Your body magnificent.

WHERE ELEPHANTS ROAM
//

Grasslands dotted with trees
Acacia, Mango,
Teak & Evergreens.
Palmettos rise against the lush backdrop,
planted by African Elephants
as they roam
Heaven's front lawn.

The gift of hospitality

A WOODEN CROSS & KITCHEN SPOON

We arrived at Ayilo Camp in Adjumani, Uganda. The trek to Ayilo was long, yet driving through the bush was pretty. When we arrived, their joy was uncontainable and the honor was overwhelming. We walked through rows of corn stalks and past the tukuls[4] with straw roof tops.

The floral and abstract prints on the dresses and head wraps pop vibrantly on the melanin of these Sudanese woman. I noticed that not only were they carrying wooden crosses into their celebratory dances, but also carried a long wooden stick with a rounded handle. I didn't think much of it until I saw this same wooden tool in the town market. I turned to Dominic, our guide, and inquired.

He said, "That is just a stirring utensil used in kitchens or cooking areas."

I responded with, "You mean it's a long spoon?" I was immensely intrigued, and remarked that many of the ladies were carrying them and the crosses into their dance circles waving them in the air.

He said, "Yes, because they want you to know that you are welcomed and they have been expecting you. It shows that they have been cooking and are extending hospitality to you."

On a Wednesday

We missed a significant day of being with people; the rains were heavy, and the thunderstorms were powerful. We had a 75-minute drive to the UN Refugee camp, only to unload and reload the van. When Africans express concern about the weather—rainstorms and potential washouts over dirt roads—everyone listens and pays attention.

We met with a group of women from the village at their clay hut church and unloaded goods and food. They gathered in a circle and wanted to pray for us before our now two-hour drive to the city, across the African bush in a storm.

We returned late Thursday morning, and the whole crew greeted us in beautiful attire and joy. There's something uplifting about their radiant smiles and the brightly colored prints adorning their gorgeous dark skin.

I realized I was wrong about "missing" a day of serving people and being with this group of refugees. One of the Dinka women said, "Thank you for coming yesterday and bringing the rain. We haven't had any water for our crops, and the day your team shows up, you came with goods and the rain."

That day taught me a lesson about provision. It taught me a little more about what it means to be faithful and obedient. It reminded me that this life of sacrificial living and being there for others is bigger than me and what I do. Yet, my obedience allows moments like these to be witnessed and for me to be part of God showing His favor. That day showed me I can never fully understand the mind of God, but I will always understand His heart and care for others.

On Language, Communication, and Honor:

I met many who spoke a minimum of four.

I realized many indigenous and tribal people are willing to learn and communicate in a way that honors another. They would even engage someone with their native tongue before using a main language. I've heard the same during my time in Mexico and the U.S. Southern Border.

Honor—that's a *language of love* we could all learn.

BISMARCK'S STORY

*"A struggle of the African
child is polygamy.*

*What man needs 10 wives
and 30 children?*

That was my father."

The women brew and sell alcohol to make ends meet—his mother became an alcoholic because of it. He was left to eat scraps and slept on cow skins with maggots.

Bismarck's story is difficult to hear, but ultimately it is one of hope and transformation. His life is a testament to the power of newfound community and support—he is now graduating University as a lawyer.

DIFFERENT PLACE,
DIFFERENT PEOPLE,
SAME JESUS —
HE MEETS THEM
WHERE THEY ARE
AND IT IS
BEAUTIFUL.

AN EXCHANGE

Many of the stories shared are stories of *resilience*.

Many tears shed are shed in *courageous vulnerability*.

Much of the hope attained was strengthened through the sacrifice of others—strangers and friends. There is beauty *in* the brokenness.

While some relationships like that of families and nations may no longer exist, there are new relationships formed that have brought healing. Tribes that were at war now find themselves living in the same UN Camps—enemies have the choice of becoming friends, and this is a wonderful and supernatural beauty.

I learned from Africans that beauty and faith are one in the same—transcendental values found in tangible relationships—an exchange of hope-filled trust.

If Africa is not Heavens front porch, I will be disappointed.

I spent two days in Doha, Qatar, and it was a dream. Thousands of Arab faces I may never meet again, with a diversity of 85 percent that allowed me to feel at ease. This land was a world of futuristic progress with a mystery of ancient times.

A DASH OF DOHA, QATAR
//

Over the Sahara,
Banners of golden bands,
Beige and pale yellows,
Kissed by an evening of navy blues.

EWW!
//

People would rather be known as expats
than immigrants.
The former is so posh & polished
while the latter is just, "eww."

Walking the maze of the ancient market, observing as only a stranger can: The Qatari people of the Arab world are free in life, and their interactions with each other are festive. There was so much to be enamored with and learned from.

CUBAN TROGON — *The freedom and spirit of the Cuban people*

CH. 05
CUBA

LIBRE

CH. 05

CUBA LIBRE

Cuba was about a shift in perspective and understanding. It taught me both to slow down and to recognize how much I still have to unlearn.

I was invited to join a small team traveling to what had long been painted as a forbidden, communist land. My propaganda-washed mind raced, while my adventurous, curious spirit shivered with excitement—and in that tension, something shifted.

I met remarkable people who didn't wish us harm or the destruction of my nation. Instead, they wanted to share a new narrative, a different way of life. They know what we think of them—what we're told by the media and by those who've left the island behind. As my new friend Joel would say, "[my team] has the opportunity to learn from true island Cubans—not those who left and now only repeat old stories in America."

In Guanabacoa, I discovered a community of Cubans cultivating something new and deeply meaningful. In my short time there, I saw how they engage with their neighbors and navigate life within what I came to understand as a "modern communist world." Joel and his team serve an aging population while bridging a generational gap, as many elders are now raising their grandchildren. Clean water, food, education, and employment aren't easily accessible, yet the partnerships they've built breathe life into these needs—creating opportunities for human flourishing. They fully understand the weight of their national and political challenges, but within their community, that pressure is eased. They care for one another.

Cuba is a land of deep intrigue. I loved its Caribbean essence—it spoke to my own roots. But more than that, Cuba expanded my understanding. It dismantled the mental and emotional walls that might have kept me from building real, honest relationships.

A SHIFT
//

I watched the spectrum of light shift
from that of seven to a welcoming of heaven
lavender strokes upon cumulonimbus
a soft embrace of mystery & wonder
as we entered the airspace of
the Pearl of Antilles—
Cuba.

LANDED
//

I walked onto a vintage movie set
tiled floors colored like
grandma's beige curtains.

It's a time capsule;
sad, pretty,
broken, tired,
wonder-filled.

LA HABANA
//

La Habana, Cuba
land of forbidden entry
locked away
loved by its people
living in a shell of former glory;
tired, worn, but still has a beautiful spirit.
"Oh what she could be"
is all I kept thinking.
Your cigars are a wonder
and the rum,
well blessed are the hands of your craftsmen.

THE STRUGGLE

History is often told from the view of the victor, but what could we learn from the other side of the story? That's one question I ask myself and one I like to share with others. For too long, the victor is assumed the hero—never the villain or the oppressor or the questionable.

While in Cuba, I had an inner struggle, a tension of knowledge and understanding, because I came to a realization that all I knew, or *thought* I knew of Cuba, was instilled by propaganda, a narrative written from the perspective of the West—the U.S. to be exact.

The other side of the story showed me that it's not as cut and dry, black and white—but most of all, that I am still learning and unlearning.

THERE SHE WAS...
//

There she was,
and I couldn't keep my eyes off her.
Dressed as a dime but tattered and worn,
she sat sadly, a shell of former glory.
Havana had been abused
you could see the history in her eyes.
It was obvious that in her prime—
damn, she was fine.
And there she was.

I asked her for a dance,
nothing fancy—
I couldn't handle the salsa she had left.
But something slow,
following the movement of the sax
and the lull of the voice
drifting from the stage at the Hotel Nacional.

I wanted to hold her close,
to listen to her stories and dreams.
I wondered if she would allow me
to be her bag valet,
to carry the baggage
my nation had thrust upon her shoulders.
Could I ease her burden,
if only for an evening?

Havana, you're a heartthrob—

would you forgive the men
who loved the thought of you,
who stole what they could from you
but never truly cared for you?

VAPOR

//

light my cigar
spirit me away
allow me to become one
with the wind.
moving upon the jet stream
I relive all of my dreams
before wisping off into eternity.

Lessons From Cuba

A lesson I took away from Cuba,
is to just be,
allow yourself to enjoy the moment at hand,
as Joel would tell us—
tranquillo.

Cubans have a gusto
that keeps them driven and proud.
They hunger for so much more.
It's not so much *poverty* as it is the *oppression*
of people and global policies.

Finca Vigía

A LESSON FROM HEMINGWAY'S HOUSE

Finca Vigía may seem like a quiet detour, but this poem is not a break—it is part of the undercurrent.

Hemingway, like the countries and people visited throughout this book, carried the tensions of violence, beauty, and fragility in his own soul. His home in Cuba becomes more than just a tourist stop—it's a portal. A reminder that even those who shaped our literary and historical memory of war were seeking refuge. In the silence of his home, among his books and fishing rods, we sense a man trying to hold together a fractured world within himself.

This poem is a quiet breath between battles, those within and in the world. A moment to reflect on legacy, on how war follows us home, and how even in the comfort of a beloved space, the echoes of conflict remain. Hope often isn't loud.

Sometimes, it's the quiet preservation of a place that once held peace for someone who knew war too well. Hemingway's home was a beautifully crafted environment for his own way to heal.

I wrote this after walking around his house and grounds in San Francisco de Paula, outside Havana. I looked out from his tower, the same view he once admired. And I wondered what ghosts he carried, and what ghosts I brought with me that day.

FINCA VIGÍA
//

I visited Hemingway's home:
I saw his boat.
I walked his grounds.
I smelled his flowers.
I took shade under trees
Planted along his garden paths.
I looked out from the same tower
Where he overlooked Cuba's beauty.

I visited Hemingway's home:
It's a shell of stories where parties once took,
Where memories were made.
It is a wonder of a home—
He made his mark on history
And here I am scouring those memories.

Driving back to Havana gave me space to meditate on legacy—Cuba's, Hemingway's, mine, ours. The visit raised quiet, but pressing questions:

What do we leave behind after conflict?

What kind of peace can take root in the soil of memory? And what allows someone to hold on to hope and wonder, even while sifting through personal or global destruction?

HAGGLES & HUBRIS

I try to stay mindful of who I am and the context I'm entering. Still, there are times that expose our blind spots—and humility always knows where to find them and extend a teaching moment.

One afternoon, while walking Havana's streets and alleyways, I laid eyes on a treasure trove of books. Immediately, I knew I had to buy a few. After negotiating a bit (cuz I love a good market street haggle) I won the bid for $15 USD. Turning to Joel in excitement, I said …

"It's a good price, right?"

His face lit up with concern because he couldn't fathom I would spend $15 for these books.

"Why not Joel?"

He then responds, "Well, I make $20 a month so that's expensive to me."

———

You never discuss money on trips, and I let my inner adventuring-self forget that rule. It was fine, and Joel was good, but I felt terrible.

A BICYCLE SEAT

Sometimes the mission is simple; a simple prayer with a simple goal. This gentleman didn't talk much, he had a gentle spirit and simple mission: to feed people in his community who can't make it out of their homes. His prayer even simpler, he chuckled and said, "I pray that God might give me a better bicycle seat."

He would deliver about 10 meals to people that desperately need it and ride about 18 miles by the time he finished his route.

Lessons From A Cuban

//

More often than not,
your mission in life is simpler than you think.
You don't need something grand & elaborate,
only simplicity & obedience.

UKRAINIAN NIGHTINGALE — *Hope, beauty, family and home*

CH. 06

Україна

UKRAINE

CH. 06

UKRAINE

I'm not sure how to lead you through this chapter. Ukraine feels too real and too raw in my life, as they continue to be bombarded by Russia.

At the time of writing this book, it's been over three years since the invasion started. I've come to befriend people there on a different level of care and love. I've been told that war changes you, and I believe that's part of what I'm sensing and feeling. While I treasure all my interactions, Ukraine won me over in a different way.

Of course, I knew of the war and had heard of the suffering, but I never imagined I would leave a part of myself there—sharing, even in the smallest way, the weight of war. I've met refugees and migrants from that part of the world, families and students who have joined the school district where I work, and others waiting for asylum at the southern border in Mexico—Ukrainians, Russians, Kazakhs, Belarusians. So it was an honor to receive a call from Andrew, the founder of

The Renewal Initiative,[1] who was following my work. We exchanged stories, backgrounds, and ideas. He asked if I would consider joining his six-man medical team headed to Ukraine, where I would serve as a first responder chaplain. I never expected my training with Coastal Crisis Chaplaincy to prepare me in so many ways for this trip—but it did.

A couple of days before our departure, I flew to D.C. and used the time as a buffer to prepare for stepping into an active war zone for two weeks. That's when the nerves really set in. Part of the preparation was something that no training could fully prepare us for: each team member was encouraged to write letters home. We took every precaution and planned out logistics, safety, and security, but the risks remained high. There was no telling what we would encounter.

I sat in a lounge in downtown D.C. with a cigar in one hand and tears filling my glass of bourbon.

My soul spilled ink onto the pages of the letters I would mail home that night. It was one of the hardest things I've ever had to do—writing farewell letters to my wife and three-year-old son.

The weight of this process made me tender. Looking back, I realized these are moments many lives never had. These are the moments many fathers, mothers, sisters, and brothers would, I'm sure, have cherished.

And in some way, maybe you'll consider this: since life is but a vapor—and I encourage you, time and again, *memento mori*, remember death—don't wait until obituary moments to speak your heart. Share the goodness of life with your loved ones—*today*.

STAGING AREA
//

Like gusts of wind, my emotions & thoughts
billow through my body.
I feel the vibrations move into my timbers.
I can only be as prepared as I know myself and
my limitations, with every new encounter.
So here I am, a day before I fly out.
A day before I set upon the jet stream,
D.C. is my staging area.
It seems, this buffer may not be enough
to sustain me.

But isn't that a fortifying truth?
Nothing—no place, no time
can sustain me.
My strength & fortification to enter the unknown
and mysteries of life can only come from the one
who sustains & fortifies;
the Father of comfort,
the originator of omniscience.

So here I stand & sit,
allowing the tremors to settle
as I speak truth & honesty about my current
state before my Maker.

LONG FLIGHT
//

The boys and I took a long flight
flying over glaciers, touching greenlit skies
before touching down on foreign lands.
We found ourselves
in the care of strangers turned kin.
Weaving our lives and stories,
bearing burdens and pain.
Sharing tears of joy and sorrow.
We would end up behind enemy lines
sharing in the risk of adventure & harrow.
Some stories just cannot be captured,
and I don't have the film to prove,
but I do know this:
It's only the favor of God
that allowed us to be bulletproof.

This isn't about heroic antics,

trust me I woke up in the middle of one night

Shook! at the sound of shingles hitting rooftops

and felt frantic.

I can't imagine what true soldiers embody,

I was only there for two weeks,

and now I'll leave it all behind and disappear.

FLOW
//

Sleeper trains
Warsaw to Kyiv
windows cracked
allowing the flow of autumn breeze.

ARRIVAL
//

It's official we are here—
the Ukrainian war zone.
Even the train tracks rattle and creek with a
weariness and agony not felt or heard before.
The evening drags on and the screeches of metal
wine through a fogged air.
Customs agents aren't smiling,
they are methodical, mechanical even.

"Who are you and why are you here?"
I consider this line of questioning a cry for help;
am I not an ambassador of another world?
An invisible, future kingdom manifested
in the present, for in my presence
I stand with the Holy Spirit.

This six man team,
nay seven for the Lord is forever with us,
is stepping into the cold darkness
with a warm light from the bosom of the Father,
the Comforter,
the originator of Grace.

Jesus is all too familiar with suffering and
in his calling to draw near,
we understand, the suffering king.
We become co-sufferers and agents of healing,
extenders of mercy thus others know God,
the one whose name is Love.

So when asked
"Who are you and why are you here?"
—we can confidently say,
"Love sent us."

It was 2am and I called my wife to check in. The night was cold, the sky was clear, and it was absolutely quiet. We paused at this camp before driving further east to the front lines. A drone squad was also staying at this location.

SILENCE
//

I sit at the pond's edge
it's quiet, unnervingly so
I can hear the hum in my head.
The sky is crisp & clear
I can see the circle of the heavens
and then reality hits
an air siren crescendos in the distance.

SOUNDS OF SOMBER
//

Boom.
Screech.
Pop.
Hum.
This is the symphony of destruction.

Most will never feel the rumble of artillery
shake the Earth.
Many will never hear sirens scream across the skies—
these are the sounds of somber.

Ukraine, oh Ukraine.
Yes over you I will mourn,
over many I will cry.

STORIES FROM THE FIELD

Vlad is frustrated and tired—worn even.

He's lost countrymen, and invaders are continually stealing their land. He holds back tears as he expresses his anger—sharing stories and telling me about the social media posts of those who abandoned all hope and now enjoy fishing trips abroad while they fight on.

Battlefield stories tear at my heart as soldiers share their horrors, desperate to release the mental and emotional strain. As a chaplain, I'm privileged to sit with them, offering a safe place for their narratives and pain to unfold.

Dr. Luke and I are off-grid, in an undisclosed location. Our six-man team was split into three groups across the front lines. As we sit with a translator, he works with mercy and compassion, offering therapy and chiropractic care. We listen. We hear stories of chemical warfare. We see photos of amputees—surgeries performed with no anesthesia and meet those same people. One soldier points to the shrapnel embedded in his arm and leg.

"Can I tell you what happened?"

"Yes, and thank you for allowing me to listen."

"I was fighting a Russian soldier—down to fists and knives. We were in the trenches when I heard a whistle in the sky. I don't know how it happened, but I pulled that fucker to my left side just as the bomb exploded. That's why I'm alive… but I still got hit with shrapnel."

One gentleman complains about phantom pain, he still feels his arm though it's gone—the body keeps count and holds trauma—it's evident in how these soldiers move.

One soldier asked Dr. Luke if he could write him a medical discharge as an American doctor. He knew that he would be sent back to battle.

An elderly woman tells her story of lying in bed when suddenly, she was awoken and thrown by the shockwave of a missile flying through her apartment.

Everything exploded, doors flew off their hinges, and she was sent flying across the room. The bomb itself didn't explode; but still, the damage done will ring well past her life.

He is a 25-year-old medic holding things together in a modest, off-the-grid rehab, tucked inside a repurposed Soviet-era building. The beds and springs held the imprints of ghosts, the windows faded, the wallpaper sagged, holding the weight of its history, and while the walls had weathered more than their share—they held firm for the need of this space. I found a moment to sit with him and ask how he was doing. This was his response.

"Physically, I'm good. Mentally, I'm changed, for good or bad I do not know."

"You see, my sister's a Baptist, but I don't believe. She always asks me about the chaplains who would visit and about the questions they asked. Then you did the same thing, and it was good. It reminded me of those conversations and I felt better when you asked the questions you asked."

We continued to have conversations for a couple days. He exhibited a hardness and strength that comes from war, yet there was a tenderness and steadiness that came from somewhere deeper.

FOR ROMAN
//

I'm sorry you were cut down
and now your absence leaves a void.
I'm sorry another man's foolishness
has left your family's heart destroyed.
I'm sorry I am powerless
to bring about peace
but please know you are missed & honored;
I look forward to hearing your story
when we meet in eternity.

I met Roman's wife, Lesia, a beautiful person who loves him dearly and misses him even more. She showed us hospitality and care one evening by opening her apartment to us and serving tea and cakes. Her name has an even more powerful meaning: *defender, helper of the people*. I think they are a power couple indeed, and we are blessed to call her friend.

Advice From the Field:

"If you hear an explosion you don't have anything to worry about, it means the bomb has already gone off so you're fine.

If you don't hear the explosion, you don't have anything to worry about because you're probably dead."

SERHII VIVCHAR

One morning, we rode out to an intersection where soldiers gathered for a meal—some coming off their posts, others heading to them. We met incredible people: soldiers, chaplains, Ukrainians, Romanians, and us Americans, all sharing a hearty meal and warm greetings.

Then we heard it—*twice*.

Artillery shells landed a mere 50 yards away. Black smoke rose, the stench of explosives filled our nostrils. We looked around, I was dumbfounded, and then everyone kept eating.

This is a reality of war—when you can, enjoy the meal and the conversation. The shadow of death is ever present at your table.

Have you ever seen a tiger cry?

**THE MERCENARY WITH
AMBER HONEY EYES**

We had heard about a trio of Colombians serving in heavy and unique positions across Ukraine. I told our team lead, Andrew, that I wanted to get in touch with this unit and crew. I felt a strong urge to reach out to my Latino brothers and encourage them in their native tongue.

Upon reaching our rendezvous point, we were warned that the road ahead was treacherous. What should have been a half-hour drive turned into an hour and a half. The Russians had taken control of the road we originally planned to take, forcing us to find a roundabout route to meet the team.

The deeper we drove, the heavier the atmosphere became. Towns that once held a mix of civilians and soldiers quickly transformed into places filled only with men of war. The scenes felt like something out of a World War II movie—jeeps, tanks, and war machines that seemed antiquated. Artillery was hidden beneath camouflage tarps. Trenches gouged the farmland, cutting deep into the hills. Tank deterrents and razor wire stretched across fields where grain once grew. Signs bearing skulls and crossbones marked the presence of landmines, rising like mile markers along the road.

Then, silence hit. No one spoke. We all felt the weight of war. A deep, unshakable dread settled over us—this could be it. No one knew our exact position, and we had entered the realm of Hades. The pothole-ridden dirt farm roads ahead only added to the tension, and we were the only souls as far as we could see.

Jeremy stood up in the van and prayed aloud—for protection, for peace, for surrender to whatever story God would write with His own hand.

In silence, we finally reached our meeting point with *El Castigador*, the Colombian I had heard about and spoken to over the phone.

I jumped out of the van and called to a lone figure standing on the dirt road.

"¡Hola, amigo!"
"¡Hola, Capellán!"

Those Spanish words immediately eased the tension. Yes—he was friendly, and I was the chaplain he had been expecting.

He led us down a short driveway behind an abandoned stone farmhouse. There was no electricity, but it provided shelter from the elements. Two more Colombians emerged and greeted us. As we walked past their hand-dug bomb shelter and stepped inside, their hospitality was unmistakable—the kind only Latinos can offer, turning even the harshest places into welcoming havens.

Seth, taking in the warmth of the moment, remarked that he was surprised this soldier's call sign was El Castigador. "He has such a kind face," he said.

With a slight smile, El Castigador responded, "It's only kind to friends."

He made us coffee over a propane camp stove, and we took time to check in on him. The doctors examined them, I prayed in Spanish, our translator prayed in Ukrainian, and another chaplain prayed in English. It was a powerful moment—

three languages lifting up prayers in the middle of a war zone, under the glow of a Maglite hanging from the rafters of this old stone farmhouse.

Later, I stepped outside to speak privately with El Castigador. He pointed to a distant hill and said, "We're seven kilometers from the front line, and there's movement surrounding this location."

I asked how he had earned the name El Castigador. He replied simply, "I'm good at my job, and that's the name my commander gave me."

For those who don't speak Spanish—
it means *The Punisher*.

I wish I could give you all the details, the stories, the photos from the day I met the Colombian Punisher in the middle of a war zone in Ukraine.

But instead, I'll leave you with a poem I wrote in the van the moment we left.

Because I can honestly say—it was a God moment to have met that latino three-man team.

And I can proudly say—a mercenary cried tears of joy and gratitude for having met with us.

THE MERCENARY WITH AMBER HONEY EYES
//

Have you ever seen a tiger cry?
Have you ever met a mercenary
with amber honey eyes?
Have you ever witnessed gentleness embodied—
a soldier of fortune wielding hospitality?

We're invited into this abandoned home
and with hands that have taken lives
on the frontlines
it is not blood which he sheds
but coffee instead.

Six Americans,
Three Colombians,
Two Ukrainians off the grid,
adjacent to farm fields
planted not with grain
but land mines.

A golden sun shines
through lavender grey rain clouds
spread over a horizon of slate blue
it kisses the rich dark earth.

In this darkened shack
a flashlight attached to the rafters
sheds light among the laughter.
Conversations across three languages
we learn of this mercenary's family,
talk of his people, discussions of why
he's in a foreign land luchando for
justice & freedom.

He calls us friends after having just met
believing we are the heroes
but the face of this Latino,
humble & inviting,
withholds the tears
of the harsh realities
to which he is fighting.

Have you ever seen a tiger cry?
Have you ever met a mercenary
with amber honey eyes?
Have you ever witnessed gentleness embodied—
a soldier of fortune wielding hospitality?

How do a handful
of men make
decisions for millions
and get to destroy
lives at will?

I dont have an answer,
but Lord,
draw an answer
and <u>make haste</u> on
your ruling.

POWERLESS
//

Powerless, that's what I am, powerless.
With all the privilege and position,
networks and connections,
it always ends with a release of them.
Borders force me to let go of the hands
I have walked with
I clasped in prayer
I gripped for courage
I took for warmth
I toasted in health
I've written poetry for—
I walk to the edge of freedom
only to cross a man-made barrier
and the hands which I've encouraged
are wrenched from mine
and left behind in an abyss of unknown
for freedom that is freely given
resides only in those born into privilege
and I can not take off my rights to bestow them
on another—
Powerless, that's what I am, powerless.

THINKING OUT LOUD I
//

Faces and names
strangers become brethren.
No longer is this a political fight over sending
funds to distant lands
these are spiritual kin, close friends.
Hell, they've gone through Hell,
and we glimpsed the shadow of death,
in some cases walked the stretch
of where others have crossed over.
I don't care what your politics are
you are now talking about my people
and if covering their lives means
I will lose one less meal in this life then so be it,
for I know we could all be force-fed
a little more humility & obedience.
My gluttonous, prideful, American life
could use a good beating.

THINKING OUT LOUD II
//

I desire peace.
I desire hope.
I desire renewal.
I desire for a people to be free—
Freed from those who have submitted themselves
to demoniacs rule.
Ukraine I am with you.
Russians I see you!
There is more to life,
than allowing yourself to be pawns
in building another's kingdom.

~~Hey~~ God,

HEY GOD I
//

Hey God,
What is renewal?
What does it mean for you Lord to be our refuge?
What is hope?

Hey God,
Where are you?
Why do you allow this to happen—
for darkness to sink its teeth into innocence for
its own pleasure?
Why have you allowed the breaking of marriages?
The loss of relationships?
The destruction of communities?

Hey God,
How long will this continue?

HEY GOD II
//

Hey God,
These are the kinds of questions
I'm confronted with,
by my inner voice and others.
My safe haven, "Blessed" and sheltered position
across the Atlantic can't give an answer.

Now, my dear reader don't you dare think
you can expound the mysteries of scripture
to reveal the mind of God,
the tension of Heaven and the sneer against
the Sovereign by our accuser Satan.

But these are honest questions,
these are honest feelings—

I fucking hate this! The loss, the pain, the angst,
the trauma, the laugh of Satan and the stench of
death, HEY GOD,
are you not angry too?!

But... when I allow my anger and hurt,
my confusion and silence to settle,
I can see through the tears,
"a light shining out of the darkness";
the hurting resting on the bosom of Christ,
the perplexed now understanding,
the despondent now hope filled.
These are the mysteries of the one
shrouded in the clouds.

Selah

My hope says, most questions won't receive an answer, but
Hey God, thank you for your willingness to listen
and step into the pain.

Не чини зла, бо зло вернеться [2]

Ukrainians seem to have such tough exteriors, historically and rightfully so—but I found they're guarding a *warmth* and *tenderness* ready to be bestowed on the world.

WOULD YOU UNLEARN AND LISTEN?
//

The thing is, I'm willing to go
where most won't go
which means I usually
see what most won't see
but the human condition is bent on believing
what it wants to believe.
So the stories I share,
and the narratives I extend
can only change a heart & mind
that's willing to upend—
willing to release what it thinks it knows
or what it once held true
willing to relinquish perceived knowledge
for something experientially new.

When my soul is tired & faith begins to fade, I turn to a God who won't turn away my questions.

CH. 07
FROM MY

JOURNAL

PART 2

Part two of my journal holds my poetic values and *God-speak*, woven into every word and theme across its pages. While it is not a chronological journey, it is honest to the spirit and state I was in. I release your heart and mind to the voice of poetry—*I pray you listen well.*

THE LANGUAGE OF ETERNITY
//

I write poetry as an act of defiance.
I write poetry as an act of healing.
I write poetry as an act of remembering.
I write poetry as an act of imitation—
for I believe God speaks in poetry
against all darkness,
in Him light and life is found.

I believe Jesus weaves words and speaks balms
to our angst and pain.

I believe His verses provoke the heart,
stir the mind,
unraveling mystery, revealing more of life.

I believe poetry is the breath of God,
the language of Jesus,
the whisper that does not fade—
hence, eternity reverberates
to the tone of His voice.

HOW DO WE FIND PEACE IN THE PIECES?
//

How do we find peace in the pieces?
The answer lies in the collectiveness—
unity through diversity,
sincerity and wholeness
that must come from outside of ourselves.
We have seen & understood
what our brokenness can & will do
how selfishness will sell a soul
for 30 shekels of silver.
Peace can make pieces whole;
truly I believe that to be wholly found in Jesus.
This isn't a religious statement
for we understand that the Middle East
has been at odds for centuries.
This isn't Americanized-political-pseudo-Christianity
fighting for false narratives
which only benefit our politics but never
the pockets of the least of these.

I truly hold to the Prince of Peace
known as Shalom
who says he stands with sinners,
not in agreement of their actions
but because only his peace can
mend the broken pieces.

Lining the scars & emptiness not with gold
but divine blood,
a sacrifice & sacrament
of Mortal & Eternal.
For wars & injustice stem from
humanity's quarrels.
Peace is found in the pieces of the
broken body Christ gave for us which in turn
allows humans a second chance
at brotherhood.

THE YEARS HAVE BEEN LONG
//

What Satan means for evil
God will turn to good
maybe that's a reason
for borders being annulled?

Trump is a bully
Biden played the pacifist
but these are the types of kings we choose
when we deny the one from Nazareth.

Maybe a global virus
would allow us to unify
but we're so caught up with self
led by fear
that we fight and further divide.

Wars and quarrels
stemming from our own tongues
humanity in crisis
the world becoming undone.

Fires and earthquakes
glaciers melting and floods
families being separated, deported
once again America splitting the nucleus—
modern atomic bomb.

White men on horseback
whipping black men—
somehow we're to believe
racism is done?

Yet, there's always more to the story
so I gain knowledge and narratives to make
amends between reality and giving others
the benefit of the doubt.

Summer of 2020 taught us nothing.
Then life turned 21,
she kept on whooping ass
and taking lives upon millions.

I'm too woke for folks that like to sleep in,
I've got too many narratives
for those that like academics
with no experience.
We're losing religion yet gaining idols,
everyone's now an expert on society
yet remain idle—
how many are actually engaging,
and making change not just for the gram?

There's a cost to keeping the status quo
so many are uncomfortable
so they're screaming for a return to normal
without realizing the costs—
social currency and keeping your tribe
isn't worth losing for another life.
Displacement and poverty grow
yet the rich have become richer
the Globe shuts down
yet they succeed in the impossible.

I want to feed a man for free
I'm some leftist liberal.
I try to protect the unborn
I'm a crazed conservative—
I don't give a damn about what you think
and the box you're putting me in.

My home and citizenship is Heaven
so I'll ascend above the rift
yet I'm also grounded:
taking the insults and screams,
for the tears, the dispelled fears,
the hugs after uplifting words of compassion
hit deep.

I'll reinstate dignity, raise up humanity,
place myself on the line
if it means another can walk over me,
not condescendingly,
but broad shouldered and a strong back
as I lift them to safety.
What'll 22, 23, 24 look like?
The verdict was once unknown, then 2025 hit
and it seems our leaders will burn our own home.

I BEAT MY CHEST!
//

If only it were laughable—
we are to be pitied.
If only it were hypocritical—
we are to be admitted.
Folly, nauseating folly
to hear the rhetoric of the president-elect.
Imperialism, Colonization, Degradation.
I decry his speech, I lament his worldview
I beat my chest in anger.

If only it were laughable—
we are to be pitied.
If only it were hypocritical—
we are to be admitted.
Folly, nauseating folly
the U.S. points a finger as Judge
to condemn the world and Sudan
yet opens Hell's doors so Gaza burns
all the more.

If only it were laughable—
we are to be pitied.
If only it were hypocritical—
we are to be admitted.
Folly, nauseating folly
Russia slays at will.

If only it were laughable—
we are to be pitied.
If only it were hypocritical—
we are to be admitted.
Folly, nauseating folly...

In Light of everything heavy...

Remember you are human.

You are not called to do everything, nor do you have the capacity to carry the weight of uncertainty and chaos, which seems to be the norm.

The rate of natural disasters and man-made pain seems to inundate all facets of society—from anxiety of coworkers to the displacement of millions and destruction of thousands.

You cannot do everything—
but you can do *something*.

Step back, know yourself, know your family, and step into the one thing you can do, the one thing you can focus on, and connect that to the next person. Together, we can all do good.

In light of everything heavy—*we lift together*.

& AGAIN
//

lessons & stories,
faces & names,
people & places,
changing my perspective
again
&
again
&
again.

IS IT A WIN?
//

I leave a war-torn country
only to begin entering
my country with a torn heart—
yes, there are many rejoicing,
but is it a win?

Is it a win when the spirit of the nation
is lost to immorality?
When a false messiah leads the masses astray
to subversive self-righteous tendencies?

Chasing convenience, pledging allegiance,[1]
clawing and fighting for surface rightness,
leaving marks and wounds on souls.

Idols lead us to destroy others;
in doing so, we destroy ourselves.

Is this a win?
Depends on the angle, but—shit—
I'm tired.

Done with looking at life in a skewed manner,
selling myself to the empire
when Jesus gave me a straight way
to the Kingdom
through mercy and love.

EXCERPT FROM

The Wood Between the Worlds
A Poetic Theology of the Cross

"But lest Christians feel superior to the chief priests who rejected Jesus as king, haven't millions of Christians since the time of Constantine done the same thing when we kick the eschatological can down the road by saying that someday the Messiah's peaceable kingdom will come, but not now? When we refuse to live as if the Prince of Peace is King of kings and Lord of lords *right now*, aren't we, too, essentially saying, 'We have no king but Caesar'? When we do this, we continue to mistake truth for the lie that the way the world stands is the way the world must be. No! Jesus died to do nothing less than re-found the world.

The trial in the Antonia Fortress ends with Pontius Pilate condemning Jesus Christ to be crucified. Pilate then washed his hands and asserted his innocence. Of course, he's not innocent. Wash his hands though he may, like Lady Macbeth, he cannot remove the damned spot of his guilt. Pilate has entered an infamy from which only the saving grace of Christ can rescue him. And therein lies Pilate's hope... and ours too. Pilate was not a monstrosity. He was a man fated to represent the world that most of us are all too comfortable with. As Miroslav Volf says, 'Pilate deserves our sympathies, not because he was a good though tragically mistaken man, but because we are not much better. We may believe in Jesus, but we do not believe in his ideas, at least not his ideas about violence, truth, and justice.'"[2]

—Brian Zahnd, *The Wood Between the Worlds: A Poetic Theology of the Cross*.

ROBIN HOOD
FROM ROBIN HOOD
BY SARA HAWKS STERLING[3]

"I have no love for the grand churchmen who feast while the poor go hungry,

but Friar Tuck—*now there's a man of God* who remembers the poor and stands with the people."

WHAT'S IN A NAME?
//

Was it a whisper that rebranded Jacob,
a wrestler of angels now called Israel?
Was it strength itself that steadied Simon's spirit,
renaming him Petros?
And Saul, who once hunted the faithful,
emerged as Paul, God's relentless apostle.

What's in a name?
Symbolism, meaning,
inner purpose rising like the tide.
The shifting, shaping of character,
what was is no longer;
one has become new.

Robin of Loxley, a thief with a creed,
his name a fortress for the voiceless in need.
Enveloped in shadows yet carries a torch,
bound to justice, so others are freed.

What's in a name?
Symbolism, meaning,
inner purpose rising like the tide.
The shifting, shaping of character,
what was is no longer;
one has become new.

In Ukraine they named me Corsair.
I come and go as the waves,
yet raise all in my wake.
Of every oppressor, I am a thorn in their side.

What's in a name?
Symbolism, meaning,
inner purpose rising like the tide.
The shifting, shaping of character,
what was is no longer;
I have become new—
a name unchained, a spirit unbound.

I HAVE NO EARTHLY KING!
//

I'm a brother in arms for the bold and unbound.
With lines taut and sails billowed by passion,
my banner stirs dread
in tyrants who fear freedom,
for I am unshackled,
a rebel against the throne—
I have no earthly King!

FLEETING
//

Time waits for no man,
and itself is fleeting.
I've had so many kairos moments,
while fighting against chronos,
witnessing every tick hit
against the backdrop of my heartbeat.

This is one reason I write:
knowing that while I'll expire one day,
the black notches on my wrist
will continue to clock time,
and the black lines on these pages
will be picked up by the future,
thus bridging the time-space continuum.

I will live on in your mind,
retelling stories in a tone you'll never know
but at least you're listening—
it's the only way to be immortal.

- CORSAIR

SPLITTING LIGHTNING
//

I will not go gently into the coming night [4]
I will rage, speak & write
against the smothering of light.

I will not allow power to outwit the wise
nor allow the sword to outdo the word.
I will split lightning
to set ablaze numb hearts & dumb minds.

I will not go gently into the coming night
I will rage, speak & write
against the smothering of light.

WHAT IS LIFE?
//

what is life except
narratives & sentences
unfolding & jumping off the tongue?

what is life except
pages yet to be turned?

what is life?

it's adventure & wonder
being birthed out of the unknown.
it's history being made
and your mark on history being left
for future generations to behold.

WOULD WE DARE TO DREAM AGAIN?
//

Would we dare to dream again?
Would we learn to dream again?

Not the kind where we throw
a penny into a wishing well,
but dreams of wonder and awe
at the majesty, goodness,
and the vastness of who Jesus is.
Dreams that speak to the saturation of our faith,
taking deep roots into our being,
because our understanding of Jesus,
our pursuit, and our reverence before Him
in waking hours,
leads us to encounter God
in the stillness of our slumber.

Would we dare to dream again?
Would we learn to dream again?

For faith requires imagination,
and imagination opens our eyes
to the mystery of God.

FALLOUT
//

The enemy of my enemy is a friend,
but anger & angst
can only fuel progression for so long.
Even then, have we truly made progress?
In the end, society deteriorates from within
as mental health declines.

MERCY
//

Jesus never met with Caesar
but he met with Death:
allowing the former to reign
and the latter to become powerless,
there is nothing to fear.

Selah.

I HAVE NO ENEMIES
//

I have no enemies
for who am I to another?
Are we not two mortals
produced of an environment
that shaped and molded our brokenness?

I have no enemies
just someone differently broken than you.

I have no enemies
for when I was an enemy of God
he not only met with me
but he ate with me,
sat across the table from me,
and while I sat and spit and poisoned his drink,
he stood up and
walked across to embrace me.

I'm told that "if we have no enemies then
life may have been lived too safely."
I can assure that is not my case.

I have no enemies
for in the angst, anger and wallowing
I find that you may just need
to be loved.

STOLEN
//

distracted and moving
feeling the disdain for injustice
in the pit of my stomach
a maelstrom of emotions—
God why?
I know the answer
still I cry
over stolen lives.

we're hit with so much news and information
no time to process
and yet time is what's the most precious,
time–precious souls
will never experience this side of eternity.

Father, will you hold them close?
Jesus, will you shed the tears?
Spirit, will you speak on their behalf
and translate those groans here?

I am holding on to the understanding
that humanity needs healing but—
human lives are being stolen,
human lives are being stolen,
image bearing lives are being stolen.

TIRED
//

I'm so tired of this shit—
the pain of shootings
the death brought on by broken humans
the savagery of destroying
my brothers & sisters
ripping them out of our stories.
Racism, bigotry, senselessness
forcing the Earth to imbibe our neighbor's blood
Satan looking on smug-faced & content
as he pulls the strings on malcontents
disrupting societies & shattering families.
I am worn and I recognize my hurting
doesn't compare to the arms that will no longer
bear loved ones—
I'm so tired of this shit.

OVERLOOKED
//

The greats become masters after death,
obituary stack niceties in polished columns,
songs sung in celebration of life on guitar riffs,
the realization of what you had after it's gone:
letters you should have sent,
words you should have said,
risks you should have taken,
life is truly too brief to be overlooked and not enjoy the present.
Missing today for fear of tomorrow.

BETWEEN SPACES
//

May I inhale Earth
and exhale Heaven—
living in between both spaces.

May I shine with hope like Helios
bringing an embrace to body & soul—
loving in between both spaces.

May I nurture in others the grit of grace
encouraging them to see & be more—
fighting in between both spaces.

May I dispel the darkness
that keep my brethren in bondage—
breaking all chains between all spaces.

MEMENTO MORI
//

Memento mori, remember death—
the ancient fathers recognized
death was otherworldly,
a foreign bane made familiar
immortals made mortal and mortality
now takes up residence as our neighbor
and this neighbor waits at our door
to usher us over
the River Styx.

The ancient fathers respected death,
understanding that if
we would focus
on the finality of our beings
we would rein in our lives
and live with such gratitude, grief and insistence
that angels would look upon us in awe
at the grit of our existence.

The ancient fathers remembered death
embraced death for themselves
lamented death for others—
not the heroic tide of idealism and idolatry
but with gritted teeth and bated breath,
knowing full well
we lose on this side of eternity
and win the war in the next.
I pray we would do the same.

EXPIRATION DATES
//

From powerful quasars containing black holes,
Death.

Illuminating plasma spheres into supernovas,
Death.

The most delicate of painted flora
fire off millions of synapses in our olfactory system,
pluck one,
Death.

The beauty of life, the first cries
of oxygen-filled lungs
now growing closer to
Death.

How fragile are we,
terracotta jars,
the apex of creation set to expire
Death.

TO THE GIVERS OF SELF

We are but stewards of stories,
a tapestry woven through
the exchanges of life's threads.
We are agents of hope, a presence of peace,
carriers of light.

If lore were written
of the dragons slain by the givers of self,
the shelves would be filled not just with valor,
but with tales of courageous vulnerability,
of compassion and care carried in our embraces,
upon our shoulders,
embossed with heaven's seal.

Darkness is dispelled;
it cannot stand nor overtake when love is shone
and shared by strangers—
for that is the imprint of God
when He befriended us.

Recognition and honor
are not what we strive for—
we move with intention
as the wind is captured in billowing sails.
We engage to lift hearts into the newness of life,
for these are gifts handed to us by a good God.

So to the givers of self,
sitting among the brethren,
in gratitude and thankfulness,
in humility and integrity,
with the strength of diverse unity,
for the common good,
for dignity and sacred worth,
for the blessing of humanity—
I am proud of you.

CH. 08

BEAUTY

HEALS

CH. 08

BEAUTY HEALS

The practice of seeking understanding often begins with movement—to take flight. It's a willingness to shift perspective, to question what is known, or step into the unknown. Yet, it also requires stillness: the discernment to remain grounded, to sit with complexity, and hold tension without rushing to resolve it.

I've learned to press into my apprehensions, to dwell in spaces where answers may never come. One of these spaces is held between beauty and brokenness. And in those moments, something deeper blooms: the ministry of presence. Sitting in community with one another—bearing the unknown, the grief, the weight—that is beauty.

Most people didn't need my answers. They didn't ask for solutions. They were renewed simply by presence. To be alone is a heavier burden than pain itself. But to be seen, accompanied, and held—this is healing. This, too, is beautiful.

In Ukraine, we found a café—an oasis of order amidst the turmoil—serving as a cornerstone of resilience. Despite the dreary rain and the muted, colorless world outside—inside, beauty breathed life into the space. The art on the walls, the comforting aroma of fresh food, and the warmth of human connection served as reminders that hope can thrive, even in the darkest places. Community and laughter within these hospitable spaces was life giving because someone decided to create a safe space for others.

At St. Michael the Archangel's Church in Kyiv, exploded war vehicles sat at the gates, their rust-colored metal starkly contrasting the church's vibrant blues and delicate iconography. Aesthetics drawing your attention to the juxtaposition of life and death. I witnessed babushkas, hands weathered by years of hardship, tending rose beds and garden plots—even after the bombs had fallen.

In South Sudan, I saw beauty resist despair. Amid scorched ground and displacement, I watched tribes carefully shape rows of corn into neat geometric patterns, cultivating life where chaos threatened to erase it. They danced, cooked, and ate in community. I sat in the shade of trees with those who had lost everything and still offered me food.

In Cuba, flowers are sold from rusted wheelbarrows beneath Cold War-era buildings, their petals soft against concrete and crumbling stone. The scent of blossoms mingled with stories of resistance and love. Beauty was the interaction of parties supporting each other in the marketplace.

I've met people who lived beauty—not as decoration, but as rebellion. Creating sanctuaries of community—where dignity flows not from policy, but from partnerships, friendships and love.

These sanctuaries—whether a café or a wheelbarrow of flowers—are more than just aesthetics. They are sacred interruptions. They ground us in something tender, real, and deeply human.

Beauty, in its simplest form—color, story, a kind smile—captures our attention. But it is through the interactions with each other where its balm can set and healing begins. Beauty does not erase pain, it makes space for it. It gives breath where breath has fled.

I've seen beauty heal. In rubble. In silence. But greater still in presence.

Beauty heals in *community*.

The beauty of poetry and words allows for richer conversations and the sharing of narratives.

Beauty heals, for it is a force that allows us to rise, rebuild, and reclaim our humanity, even in the face of destruction.

Beauty is the heart of God etched in kindness and compassion.

Beauty heals, for it is the face of God allowing us to reclaim salvation even in the face of death.

I've stood at the edge of contrasts: life and death, light and darkness, ruin and wonder. I no longer seek the need to explain these tensions. I honor them, and in doing so, thread these moments for stronger bonds.

On this side of eternity, war will clash with peace. Forgiveness will wrestle with grief. But even there—*especially there*—beauty endures. Even the flora find ways to grow through concrete.

These questions now live in me, and I allow them to lead me in curiosity to another: What is the potential for beauty to birth hope? Let us find out. Can the grotesque lead to more life? Let us seek this out. These are the seeds I leave with you.

Let beauty lead you home.
Let it interrupt your despair.
Let it teach you to see and love again.

Allow beauty to catch your attention and lead you to *more*.[1] Beauty heals, for it is rebellious, hopeful, and love-filled.

Let beauty lead you *home.*

I HAVE SEEN THE LORD WORK IN MAGNIFICENT WAYS AND INTERACT WITHIN A CONTEXT THAT MOST WILL NEVER KNOW.

THANK YOU

To my wife, Sarah—for giving me the strength and encouraging me to take flight, even at the cost of my time away from you and our wonderful son.

To my son, JMD—while you may not be able to read this book yet, and you may not fully comprehend the times I am away from you, I love your resilience, your kindness, and your renewing embrace upon my return. I hope that in times of uncertainty, you will always remember and internalize that "Daddy is helping people, because it's what we do."

To the G&T crew—for joining me in life, friendship, and in the editing and formatting of this book.

To the Grace City Church community—staff, pastors, and leadership team—for your encouragement and for creating a space for healing and growth.

To Empower One, Mike Congrove, and David Kaya—for paving the way to Africa and teaching me so much through your life and leadership. True Elders for generations!

To Colin Kerr—your trust, friendship, and your role in instigating calculated risk-taking.

To Dr. Andrew Moroz and The Renewal Initiative—for taking a chance and inviting me to join you upon the jet stream to Ukraine. Who knew this friendship would flourish?

To the Ukrainian team—we are brothers, and it is a joy and pleasure to know you. Thank you for building into me. Seth, Luke, Zach, Adam, Serhii—you guys are servant leaders and incredible examples of entering darkness with both grit and grace.

To those whose stories I carry and retell—to those who will never read of your impression and imprint on my life—I hope this book honors you.

Thank you.

NOTES

Introduction
1. *Upon the Jet Stream I:* This opening poem references Jonah, a Hebrew prophet and Book found in the Scriptures.

From My Journal: Part I
1. The line, "whisked away by The Spirit of God", draws from the Greek word (πνεῦμα) Pneuma, meaning Spirit, Breathe or Wind. This symbolism is woven into the book's title and reflects the unity and interaction between the physical and spiritual—being led by the pneuma, listening to pneuma while flying upon pneuma.
2. *Emmaus Road:* Inspired by the Gospel of Luke, Chapter 24:13-33.

Send Me to Hell
1. Christians are called to enter places of darkness to share light, grace, and love—but this calling is personal and should be discerned through conversation with Jesus and sensitivity to the Spirit of God.
2. Training under Chaplain Rich Robinson, Coastal Crisis Chaplaincy, Charleston, SC: crisischaplaincy.org
3. *Saint Martin of Tours* is regarded as the first chaplain.
4. The chaplain virtues in *Keeper of the Cloak* are rooted

in scripture, echoing Matthew 25:35-36—ministering to the hungry, imprisoned, and sick. Chaplaincy embraces this calling outside traditional church walls, providing care and spiritual support in often unseen places.

5. Quote from *Formed and Filled*—a two-part sermon series on Genesis 1 by Pastor David Kite, Grace City Church, North Charleston, SC. Listen at: thegracecity.com/teaching/formed-and-filled-genesis-1-1-13

Geopolitics & Poetry

1. *Operation Carlota:* Cuban military involvement in Angola and the wider Cold War context.

2. *First Raise a Flag: How South Sudan Won the Longest War but Lost the Peace* by Peter Martell.

3. Ukraine invasion by Russia: war.ukraine.ua

Welcome to Africa

1. Empower One: empower-one.org

2. United Nations in South Sudan: southsudan.un.org

3. *Postcards from Babylon: The Church In American Exile* by Brian Zahnd.

4. An African mud hut with a straw roof top.

Ukraine

1. The Renewal Initiative: renewalinitiative.com

2. Ukrainian proverb: "Не чини зла, бо зло вернеться" — "Do not do evil, for evil will return."

From My Journal: Part II

1. *Is It A Win?*: I wrote this poem while sitting in a café in Warsaw, Poland. We had just arrived after leaving Kyiv. As news of the American election played on the screens, I pressed play on Sticks & Stones by Kings Kaleidoscope—and the ink spilled. Kings Kaleidoscope, Sticks & Stones, The Beauty Between (BadChristian Music, February 23, 2017), audio recording.

2. *The Wood Between the Worlds: A Poetic Theology of the Cross* by Brian Zahnd. Cited Miroslav Volf, *Exclusion and Embrace* (Nashville: Abingdon Press, 1996), 276

3. Quote from *Robin Hood* by Sara Hawks Sterling, 1921 Sterling printing.

4. *Splitting Lightning*: Inspired by Dylan Thomas' *Do Not Go Gentle into That Good Night*.

Beauty Heals

1. A note on the three transcendentals: Goodness, Truth, and Beauty—universal qualities that draw us closer to the divine and to one another.

Photography

The photos used in *Upon the Jet Stream I*, *Send me to Hell*, *For Roman*, and *Beauty Heals* provided by Lesia Suvalko.

Pseudonyms

Some names have been altered to protect the identity of those in hostile areas.

www.ingramcontent.com/pod-product-compliance
Lightning Source LLC
Chambersburg PA
CBHW041216130526
44582CB00025BA/32